THE BEANFIELD

BREACH

Breach is theatre-makers Billy Barrett and Ellice Stevens, and video artist Dorothy Allen-Pickard. It has been called 'a young company with a strong creative identity' by The Stage, and won the 2015 Total Theatre Award for an Emerging Company. *The Beanfield* is Breach's first show, made in collaboration with four associate performers whilst all were students at Warwick University.

THE BEANFIELD

DIRECTED BY
Dorothy Allen-Pickard (video)
Billy Barrett (live)

MADE AND PERFORMED BY
Billy Barrett
Grace Holme
Anna-Himali Howard
Max Kennedy
Ellice Stevens
Tom Wright

LIGHTING DESIGN
Ethan Hudson

PRODUCED BY
Amanda Fawcett

THANKS TO
Nicola Baldwin, Emma Beverley, David Byrne, Freshblood New Writing, Institute of Advanced Teaching and Learning, Antoine Marinot, Chris Maughan, Will Monks, Moritz Müller-Guthof, Jake Orr, Megan Vaughan, New Diorama Theatre, and all the donors to our crowdfunding campaign.

PERFORMANCE DATES

Warwick University Humanities Studio: 8th-10th May 2015

Warwick Arts Centre (Warwick Student Arts Festival): 23rd June 2015

Theatre503: 25th-26th July 2015

theSpace, Edinburgh Festival Fringe: 6th-22nd August 2015

New Diorama Theatre: 18th-19th October 2015

National Student Drama Festival, Scarborough: 19th-22nd March 2016

Salisbury Arts Centre (Theatre Fest West): 24th March 2016

Pound Arts Centre (Theatre Fest West), Corsham: 26th March 2016

Home, Manchester: 31st March-2nd April 2016

Battersea Arts Centre, London: 4th-21st April 2016

Birmingham Repertory Theatre: 26th-27th April 2016

The Wardrobe Theatre, Bristol: 28th-30th April 2016

The Bike Shed Theatre, Exeter: 3rd-7th May 2016

Supported using public funding by

LOTTERY FUNDED | **ARTS COUNCIL ENGLAND**

Foreword – Andy Worthington

A generation ago, on June 1st 1985, a convoy of vehicles travelling through the English countryside to Stonehenge to establish what would have been the 12th annual Free Festival was set upon with violence on a scale that has not otherwise been witnessed in modern times in the UK.

The festival – a huge, anarchic settlement that had occupied the fields opposite Britain's most famous ancient monument for the whole of June, attracting tens of thousands of visitors – was a thorn in the side of Thatcher's authoritarian government. As were the travellers who made up its core – some of whom had also been causing trouble by protesting proposals to host US cruise missiles on UK soil. Following the women of Greenham Common who had set up the first protest camp, travellers and green activists established a second camp at Molesworth in Cambridgeshire, which was intended to be the UK's second cruise missile site.

This camp was broken up with the largest peacetime mobilisation of the military in February 1985, and the convoy was then harried until the 1st of June, when the final showdown between travellers and the authorities took place. Unknown to the travellers, around 1400 police from six counties and the Ministry of Defence were sent to Wiltshire to 'decommission' the convoy – which consisted of around 500 men, women and children.

The police were thwarted in their efforts to arrest the majority of the convoy via a roadblock near the A303, seven miles east of Stonehenge. The travellers then occupied a pasture field and an adjacent beanfield, establishing a standoff that was only broken late in the afternoon. Under instructions from on high, the police invaded the fields en masse, and violently assaulted and arrested the travellers – smashing up their vehicles to try and make sure this new nomadic movement could never function again.

Successive waves of legislation – the Public Order Act of 1986 and the Criminal Justice Act of 1994 – largely destroyed Britain's traveller community, and criminalised impromptu gatherings like the Stonehenge Free Festival. There were, however, fascinating eruptions of dissent along the way – in particular via the rave scene of the late eighties and early nineties, and the road protest movement that was a direct descendant of the Free Festival. Unable to travel freely, protesters rooted themselves to a fixed spot, occupying land regarded as sacred and, in many noteworthy cases, living in trees in an effort to prevent road-building projects from taking place.

Widespread dissent made another resurgence at the end of the 20th and start of the 21st century through the anti-globalisation movement. The heavy-handed efforts to suppress it – and a renewed onslaught on civil liberties in the wake of the terrorist attacks of September 11th 2001 – means we are now in danger of forgetting what we have lost in terms of our freedoms of movement, of gathering, of dissent and of celebration.

So I was delighted when early in 2015, the theatre director Billy Barrett and filmmaker Dorothy Allen-Pickard got in touch and invited me to join them at the Beanfield, to act as a consultant as they filmed recreations of the event. It was my first visit to this iconic site, although I had passed it many times on the A303. While police sirens passed us by, we spent a few hours filming and reflecting on the events of the day – ironically, given the convoy's environmental leanings, at a small solar farm, where thirty years before there would only have been burning vehicles and bleeding travellers.

It was a powerful afternoon, summoning up some of the ghosts of that distant day when the law failed, with a collective focus on why it needs remembering. I commend all those involved in this production for keeping the memory alive.

Andy Worthington is an investigative journalist, campaigner, and author of The Battle of the Beanfield *and* Stonehenge: Celebration and Subversion.

First published in 2016 by Oberon Books Ltd
521 Caledonian Road, London N7 9RH
Tel: +44 (0) 20 7607 3637 / Fax: +44 (0) 20 7607 3629
e-mail: info@oberonbooks.com
www.oberonbooks.com

Copyright © Breach, 2016

A catalogue record for this book is available from the British
Library.

PB ISBN: 9781783197330
E ISBN: 9781783197347

Cover photography by Richard Davenport at the New Diorama

Images, cover and text design by Breach

Printed, bound and converted
by CPI Group (UK) Ltd, Croydon, CR0 4YY.

THE BEANFIELD

Notes on the Text

Just as *The Beanfield* doesn't claim to offer a thorough, or even accurate, account of the Battle of the Beanfield and the contentious modern history of public gatherings at Stonehenge (for which Andy's books and the documentary *Operation Solstice* will be of more use), this text can hardly hope to capture the show itself – which exists between film and performance, in a space created and shared with its audience.

As well as being an approximate record of a show then (and it feels important to the politics of the project that it is, in one sense, a record), this book inevitably exists as its own thing – to be experienced on its own terms. With this in mind, we've minimised interruptive stage directions within the text – with the exception of the final section '02.45', which, as the most 'theatrical', seems to benefit from them. If you're interested in the other ways that *The Beanfield* works onstage, these notes could be useful to consider whilst reading:

- The set consists of a 4 x 4m square of Astroturf – bright green and clearly artificial. Behind this, a line of six black chairs on which the performers sit when they're not speaking, and a large screen onto which video is projected throughout the show.

- The cast read the opening 'Emails' section from printed sheets of paper, standing in a line and wearing their own clothes. After the final email is read out, the performers change onstage into contemporary festival gear: metallic shorts, flower crowns, neon t-shirts, bumbags, raincoats, glitter, face paint.

- During the 2015 solstice sections, the cast stand in a semi-circle on the Astroturf facing the audience – 'you'. In each of these fragments, the number of performers diminishes by one, and those who don't take part remain seated. A slash (/) denotes a point of interruption, and a hyphen (–) indicates a pause. The Google Maps onscreen depict the location – but not, of course, the date or time – of the action described.

- During the interviews about the battle, the performers ask their questions onstage facing the screen, between the recorded responses. Footage of the intervewees is intercut with documentation of the cast's research and preparations for the re-enactment:

  - 'Nick (Journalist)': The cast watch the documentary Operation Solstice.

  - 'Ruwan (Ex-Police Officer)': Billy, Ellice and Tom change into police costumes.

  - 'Carol (Ex-Traveller)': The cast watch YouTube footage of the Stonehenge Free Festival. Anna, Grace and Max change into traveller costumes.

  - 'Nottingham Medieval Re-enactment Society': The cast rehearse their own re-enactment sequences (both onscreen and onstage), and make props and costumes.

- For the 'Landowner' section, the phone ringing interrupts Ellice mid-sentence. She takes out her phone onstage and answers it as the Wiltshire landowner – speaking between Dorothy's recorded half of the conversation. After hanging up she sits back down, and Dorothy's conversation with Grace continues onscreen.

- Just before the 'Re-enactment' section, the performers leave the stage and all lights come down, leaving only the screen visible.

[Cruel Summer – **Bananarama]**

Emails

Billy: Dear English Heritage

I'm the director of a historical re-enactment society. We're planning to re-enact the Battle of the Beanfield, which took place exactly thirty years ago this June. The violent clash between New Age travellers and police resulted from you taking out an injunction around Stonehenge, along with the National Trust and local landowners, to prevent the annual Free Festival.

Given your own programme of battle re-enactments and involvement in the events of 1985, I'm wondering if you'd like to work with us and make this an official English Heritage event. We'd love to re-enact the battle at Stonehenge itself.

I look forward to hearing from you.

Billy

Dorothy: Dear Nick

I've just realised it's over three years since I interviewed you about the phone hacking scandal! I'm still making films, and am currently working with a historical re-enactment society on a project about the

BREACH

standoff at Stonehenge in 1985. We watched a documentary on it and saw you were there as a reporter.

I'll be filming a reconstruction by the company, hopefully at Stonehenge. I'm getting in touch because we're looking for a witness to come with us and act as an advisor.

It would be brilliant to have you involved.

All the best

Dorothy

Tom
(as Nick): Dear Dorothy

Good to hear from you. I like the sound of the Stonehenge project and I'd be happy to meet up and talk to you about it. However, whilst I have some powerful memories, I may not be the right person for the visit. I'd suggest you ask Andy Worthington instead, who wrote a book about it.

On a small point, do you know the actual location of the Beanfield? It was quite far from Stonehenge – just the arbitrary point at which the police stopped the convoy en route. Maybe you know that, but it sounds like you think the battle was actually at Stonehenge.

Good luck

Nick

Ellice: Dear Ruwan

I'm part of a historical re-enactment group planning to recreate the Battle of the Beanfield. I came across your Amazon review for Andy Worthington's book, which suggested you were involved as a police officer.

Would it be possible to interview you about your experience there?

All the best

Ellice

Max
(as Ruwan):   Hi Ellice

More than happy to assist and offer some thoughts. Those were not days to be proud of, neither at the 'Stones' nor policing the Miners' Dispute, which we were called away from to police Wiltshire on that long hot summer of 1985.

Yours sincerely

Ruwan

Grace: Dear Carol

I think my parents Martin and Anna Holme knew you from Christian volunteering at Glastonbury in the early nineties? I'm part of a historical re-

enactment group at Warwick planning to reconstruct the Battle of the Beanfield for the thirty year anniversary. When I told my parents about it they said they knew a traveller who was there and I was amazed! My dad said he had you on Facebook, so I looked you up.

Strangely enough the day we began our research, we were also involved in a protest here at Warwick University which was violently broken up by the police. They sprayed us with CS gas – the first time it's been used on students on a UK campus – and threatened us with a taser.

*Audio recording from Warwick For Free Education's occupation of the Senate House foyer, 3rd December 2014. Audible between screams and the clicking of a taser gun: 'Oh my god'... 'Stay where you are'... 'What is happening?'... 'He's got a taser'... 'What the fuck are you doing?'... 'Stay off my friend'... 'Police brutality'... **Grace**'s voice: 'that was a fucking joke – we were sat there having a discussion!'*

Would you be up for an interview with me about your experiences? It would really help me with my performance.

Warm regards

Grace xx

Anna
(as Carol): Hi Grace

Ah, I thought you might be Martin's daughter. Yes I would love to help – I saw

and shared the uni protest vids. Bless you, it's not easy to keep calm and peaceful in the face of such violence.

Love to your Mum and Dad.

Carol xxx

Billy: Hi Kate

This is slightly out of the blue, but am I right in saying you're part of a historical re-enactment group?

Dorothy and I are currently making a theatre and film piece about the Battle of the Beanfield (see Wikipedia link below). She's going to film me and the cast attempting to re-enact it, then onstage we're going to try and give our audience an experience of being at the Stonehenge summer solstice in 2015.

We keep telling people that we're a historical re-enactment group, to sound legitimate – but we actually have no idea how it works. So we're interested in talking to real re-enactors to find out – would you be up for having a chat?

Thanks

Billy

Anna
(as Kate):   Hi Billy

This sounds interesting. Sure, I know lots of medieval re-enactors in Nottingham who

BREACH

would be happy to speak with you. We have a meeting next week, so could Skype you then?

Kate

Dorothy: Dear Andy

I wrote to you in December concerning a project about the Battle of the Beanfield that I'm working on. The journalist Nick Davies gave me your contact details. I'm getting in touch again to see whether you'd had the chance to consider joining us for this project?

All the best

Dorothy

Max
*(as Andy)***:** Hi Dorothy

My apologies, I meant to reply earlier. I'd be happy to be involved – it's not every day someone asks you to go to the Beanfield. I've never been to the site itself, but drew up some maps for the book – pick me up at Aylesbury and I can try and help you find it.

Best

Andy

BREACH

Ellice *(as*
English Heritage): Dear Billy

Thank you for taking the time to contact English Heritage South West. I have passed your details onto our events team; they will contact you directly if any opportunities become available for this event.

If you have any further questions please contact our Customer Services Department on customers@english-heritage.org.uk.

Kind regards

████ ██████

Event Admin Manager
Customer Services

[*Solar* – Cosmo Sheldrake]

I rose up at the dawn of day

Get thee away, get thee away

Pray'st thou for riches? Away

I rose up at the dawn of day

Get thee away, get thee away

This is the throne of mammon grey

Away

I rose up at the dawn of day

Get thee away, get thee away

Pray'st thou for riches? Away

I rose up at the dawn of day

Get thee away, get thee away

This is the throne of mammon grey

Away

20:31

Ellice: It's 8 pm

Billy: Let's make it 8.31

Ellice: OK, it's 8.31 pm. On the 20th of June, 2015

Tom: So it's early evening, and you step out of the hired minibus and look around. Cars speed past. The blur of the cars

Grace: The sound of sheep in a nearby field. Blue sky, still warm but with a light breeze. You're fully kitted up. Face paint, / Aztec print bumbag

Anna: Aztec print bumbag

Ellice: Temporarily some sort of whimsical festival fairy, and you can already feel glitter in every orifice. Your friends pile out of the doors behind you, stretching out pins-and-needles

Anna: Well they're sort of friends, but some are like friends of friends, colleagues

Max: Right, basically whoever joined the Facebook event. And you brush some crumbs off your lap, from the Ginsters scotch egg bar you were eating in the hot van

Grace: Someone passes you your bag from the back of the minibus. You unzip it, and pull out a glass bottle of vodka

Ellice: It's Vodkat, £4.99

BREACH

Grace: Yes, and you decant it into a plastic bottle as per the rules on the English Heritage website, for their 'police managed access' to the Stonehenge summer solstice

Billy: You're the sort of person who reads those rules

Max: You chuck the empty glass bottle into a patch of nettles by the road

Grace: No

Ellice: Or you don't, because you're not the sort of person who litters

Max: OK you don't, you put the empty bottle back in your bag, and the driver gives you a weary smile as he pulls away. And he promises to meet you in the same spot at 6am

–

Billy: You cross the road to join your group, who are all talking about the sunrise, because apparently the sunrise is like, the thing, it's why people go. And someone's describing it like it's going to be this big yellow semi-circle coming up over the line of the horizon, like *The Lion King*

Tom: Yeah like *The Lion King*, like Simba being held up by Rafiki

Ellice: 'Aahh Savenyaah'

Grace: Yeah, to find some higher, dance-induced state of consciousness

Anna: You've spent the whole winter wearing black and being all ironically detached, acting like you don't give a shit

Grace: Or being paid to act like you give / too much of a shit

Anna: Too much, and tonight you just want to do something completely in earnest – try and not laugh at the fact that this is probably going to be some awful hippy bullshit, and just embrace it. You know, that same sun that was there a year ago

Tom: Thirty years ago

Billy: A thousand years ago. The same sun that those medieval druid people worshipped when they came to sacrifice, sort of, chickens, or maybe lambs

Max: Virgins

Tom: Or something equally plausible. And you're hoping to have this moment of warmth and profoundity

Anna: Profundity

Tom: Profundity and like earthy connection where you're all together, and you'll look at each other and just / be like

Ellice: Be like ... this is so *real*

–

Grace: You're walking along the roadside now

Tom: The blur of the cars

Grace: Pulling the seed heads off tall grass. The stones in the distance a row of tiny grey teeth

Ellice: One of your friends – the type who un-self-consciously wears harem trousers as casual daywear – is skipping ahead. She's playing a djembe

Max: Of course she's got a fucking djembe

Grace: Not that there's anything wrong with playing the djembe if it's, you know, your traditional cultural instrument

Billy: But it's not her traditional cultural instrument

Tom: Whatever, she likes playing it. So you run a few paces to join the group. You picture what you must all look like from the outside

Grace: From above: the view from a drone. Swarming like ants, over a green square cut by a grey razor-blade

Tom: Nice, exactly, like a razor, the blade of the dual carriageway slicing through the fields

Billy: And image follows image like this as you walk as a group, a pack, a pride

Ellice: Shot from the front, you think you might look like an underground electro band

BREACH

Billy: The opening credits of a gritty youth drama

Grace: Or a spoken word poetry collective, and you try to hold the moment in time

Ellice: That instantness of the instant

Grace: Cement it in your mind to remember later.

Nick Davies (Journalist)
Guardian offices, London

Nick: OK, we're all ready – Billy, shoot. Somebody shoot.

Billy: Right, OK, so how did you come to be at the Battle of the Beanfield – and what did you see there?

Nick: In the summer of 1985, I was the Home Affairs Correspondent at *The Observer*. And I could see that there was the potential for a really nasty bust-up between the convoy trying to go to the festival at Stonehenge, and the Wiltshire establishment including the police trying to stop them. So on the Friday of that week, I went down somewhere west of Wiltshire, found a little section of the convoy, and started travelling with them. So I was with the convoy as a whole when it met up in Savernake Forest that Friday night, and I was with them on the Saturday morning as they started travelling towards Stonehenge and were stopped, and broke through the hedge into this farmer's beanfield.

And so then I was one of the very few outsiders when the fighting started. And what I saw was an act of organised bullying, some of it really quite vicious, where grown men carrying sticks and riot shields and helmets to protect themselves attacked men, women and children who were not armed and who were almost defenseless. Flight in their vehicles was their only form of defence, and I saw some of their homes catching fire, and burning, and I saw some of them being hit. And all of them, I think, were arrested.

Billy: Yes, you said in your email you have some powerful memories from the day. And how did you react at the time to seeing all of this happen around you?

Nick: When all of the fighting stopped and everybody had been arrested, I went and found a tree stump to sit on and scribbled out a story in my notebook, and I went and found this farmhouse that was a few minutes walk away, and I gave them ten quid to use their phone.

And I called the office and I told them what had happened and I filed my story, and then I called my partner, and I tried to tell her what had happened – and unusually for me, I started crying. Because it was extremely upsetting to see essentially vulnerable people being attacked by grown men with big sticks and riot shields and helmets – it was an utterly uneven battle. And I was very clear in my own mind that it need never have happened. There were ways of handling the situation that did not involve violence.

And then there was this kind of slightly surreal moment where some officers came away from a bus with this guy between them with blood running down his face, and he looked very young. And I thought, if they've beaten up a child, then I need to know that he's a child. So weirdly, as a reporter, I had to say to this poor lad who was bleeding and in some pain, 'how old are you?' And he said eighteen. I think... I think generally there was a feeling of horror in the field.

Billy: And is that horror something that you still think about today?

Nick: No ... so I mean, some of it was strong enough that bits have stayed in my memory, but it is a long time ago now, isn't it? It's thirty years, it was '85. So it's not something I would think about every day. I think that for the travellers in the convoy, it was genuinely traumatic. Lots of them had their homes destroyed, quite a few of them were physically injured. I think all of them were arrested, and facing trial and punishment – although that subsequently all collapsed – and I think it had a very, very destructive effect.

Billy: So what advice would you give to someone who was directing a historical re-enactment of the battle?

Nick: That's a very ... er, the trouble is, that's not my skill. So I don't know that I've got any very sensible thing to say. What sort of thing are you asking me to think about?

Billy: Sorry, er – what sort of problems should *we* be thinking about, when we try to reconstruct what happened?

Nick: Well, the immediate problem would be one of resources. You'd need 500 people if you were going to reconstruct it, because I think there were 400 ... 450 people in the convoy – in fact, it's far more than that, because there were hundreds of police officers. You'd need a thousand extras if you were actually going to reconstruct it. So that would be difficult.

There was also a great deal of damage and destruction – so they destroyed the farmer's field, but there were also lots of the vehicles that were in flames with smoke pouring out of them. It would be a very expensive thing to do. There was also a lot of violence, which I suppose isn't terribly easy to stage without hurting people. So I mean, apart from the enormous number of people, the expense, the damage, and the injury ... no, it should be quite easy for you to do.

BREACH

20:45

Grace: 8.45 pm

Max: Yeah, so about fifteen minutes later

Ellice: It's about fifteen minutes later, and you've reached the entrance to the field, where there's this snaking queue of people

Grace: Snaking yeah, like a festival queue, crowds crammed together to be stopped and searched

Ellice: You're squeezed into a line, single file. Your friends are behind you, and in front a guy wearing what looks like a medieval wizard costume

Anna: But obviously like fancy dress nylon

Tom: And your body is ordered by metal barriers that press, cold, against your elbow

Ellice: You see men and women at the end of the line dressed in hi-vis jackets and black boots with walkie-talkies. You hear a dog barking, and immediately think to the baggy suspended in a pot of hummus in your rucksack, in its little lentilly hiding place

Grace: Chickpeas

Ellice: What?

**Grace/
Anna:** Hummus is chickpeas

Ellice: OK, chickpea hiding place. You see a stranger

Tom: A man, being marched off by the police – bit of an obvious one, white guy with dreadlocks down to his waist

Grace: His hands are pressed behind his back

**Tom/
Max:** Shit

Ellice: You feel your heart rate go – you don't want to be banned from working with kids. Not that you'd ever actually want to work with kids

Anna: Obviously, they're annoying

Ellice: So annoying, but bodies are already moving forward now, one-by-one-by-one-by-one

Tom: Six bodies

Ellice: You picture the baggy

Tom: Five bodies

Anna: 'It's like a fucking airport,' says nylon druid

Tom: Four bodies

Max: Alright, Gandalf

Tom: Three bodies

Grace: You take off your rucksack and hold it in front of you, to look helpful and compliant

Anna: With your eyes you're saying, 'I *love* to comply'

Tom: Two bodies

Grace: You can do this

Anna: Nope, can't do this

Ellice: And you're up – and you're wondering whether it would be too much to pat the sniffer dog.

Max: You hand over your rucksack. Give security an 'alright mate'

Ellice: Though you don't know if you can ever quite pull off 'mate'

Anna: You definitely can't pull off 'mate', and you can feel that stretching your face into what you hoped was a casual smile is actually really unconvincing

Grace: He pulls out the empty glass bottle, gives you a look ... and chucks it in a black bin liner

Tom: You breathe softly and count the beats in your chest. 1, 2, 3, 4, f –

Ellice: And he hands you your bag back and waves you on, telling you

Anna: Instructing you

Ellice: To have a good time.

Ruwan Uduwerage-Perera (Ex-Police Officer)
Greenham Common, Newbury

Ellice: First question: can you just tell me a bit about yourself, and what your role was on that day, during the Battle of the Beanfield?

Ruwan: It was – hmm – let me think. I was a twenty-three-year-old police officer. The previous week I'd been up in Nottingham, I believe, on the miner's dispute. We were called back because we were told that this year Wiltshire was going to put an end to the festival, the yearly festival. All the previous years I'd been involved in policing the festival – and quite frankly it used to be quite fun.

But this year was the year it was going to stop, and it wasn't a coincidence that the miners' dispute was going on at the same time, because we had a … the public were probably used to that style of policing, they'd been used to a heavy-handed, army-style of policing for almost a year regarding the miners. And so to now use it at the – on the New Age travellers, probably wasn't initially going to be an issue.

So we were conscious of the fact that as we came back and we were told we were going to be deployed onto the New Age travellers and that the concert wasn't going to go ahead this year, that there was going to be a showdown. We knew that was going to happen.

Ellice: That's really interesting. Could you go into that in a bit more detail – the similarities between the Beanfield and the miners' strike, and how the police operated during those events?

Ruwan: There was huge similarity in the sense that they were both seen as criminal – it was a criminal act that was about to happen. There was actually, I think, a slight difference in the sense that, I think, in hindsight looking back at it now, there was a nobility that was added to the miners that wasn't given to the New Age travellers. The reality was that a whole myth was built up around the New Age travellers to demonise them, and that included – as we've seen with Gypsy and Roma communities – it's literally down to turning them into sub-humans.

So to be able to do the most horrendous things to someone, you have to actually dehumanise them. And that certainly was the case with the New Age travellers – that wasn't the case with the miners.

Ellice: And how were the police behaving that day?

Ruwan: There was not much discipline – it was ill-disciplined. I can remember on the van, the public order van that I was on, my colleagues actually criticising the officers who were in there – because they were bound to be ill-disciplined because they weren't up the right standard, to be ripping people – destroying people's homes and arresting people. So there was a frustration, a weird frustration about that.

Ellice: In our re-enactment, I'm going to be playing a police officer. What advice would you give me for my performance?

Ruwan: I think if anyone's playing the part of a police officer, they need to almost be schizophrenic. In the sense that between themselves, the police officers themselves, there would have been the usual banter and good humour or whatever, and if – and it happened numerous times, so many times I can't even remember – one of the New Age travellers would suddenly come into the vicinity, as quick as that, that person would be treated in the most inhumane way. And then we'd go back to the laughter and the humour.

Ellice: And in your opinion, was that day always going to end violently?

Ruwan: When there's a large concentration of police officers who are able to devolve their responsibility onto a chain of command going up, they will always end up in violence. It was inevitable. The police were fully kitted up to be involved in a violent situation – and I hate to say this, but if you give the people the weaponry to use, and then put them in a volatile situation, they will use it.

Ellice: Do you think any of the other police officers who were there still think about it?

Ruwan: I don't think they do. Most police officers would say they joined for all the right reasons. But how on earth can they go in and do the things that we did – destroy people's homes, split families, take children away, drop the children into social services, split the parents up? Some were sixty, seventy, eighty miles apart. The children – we didn't even know where they were going.

Now how on earth can we sit back and say that was appropriate? It just wasn't. And not one person was convicted – literally hundreds of people arrested, and no one convicted. And to this day, there's never been an inquiry.

21:15

Grace: It's just gone nine

Max: 9:02 pm

Grace: OK, so you've been in for about half an hour, and different crowds of people swarm around and past you

Anna: More nylon wizards

Tom: Morris dancers

Grace: White girls wearing bindis

Anna: Always

Tom: A million pairs of eyes

Grace: And you're thinking, how is it possible that every single person here has like their own stories, or – more like, their own

Tom: Their own qualia

Max: Who's / qualia?

Grace: What?

Tom: It's like your specific subjective personal experience of something – like I can't experience your experience, and / you can't experience my experience

BREACH

60

Grace: You can't experience my experience, OK
so let's just say 'specific subjective personal
experience' then

Anna: And as you're thinking about this, you feel like
a bit like you're drowning in the crowd. You
flash back to the baggy in the hummus, and
wonder whether you should actually be doing
drugs tonight, because recently you've been
waking in the middle of the night to like, heart
palpitations

Tom: It's nothing

Max: Palpitations makes it sound extreme, like a
heart attack

Grace: Right, but that is basically what it is,
palpitations

Anna: And in those moments you feel like your room
is closing in on you on all four sides, and you
can't, er

Tom: It sounds extreme, and it's sort of nothing, but
it's like you can't breathe sometimes – in bed

Max: In the city

Anna: On the underground

Max: And you can't help but think that even though
amphetamines are obviously really lovely and
fun, they're probably not really going to help

–

Grace: Your friends have settled on a brown scratchy carpet pulled over the grass, crowded around a beardy man playing a guitar. You tune in and realise he's singing some sort of political folk song, which you're semi on-board with

Max: But it's really clunky and it has too many syllables in each line, like trying to cram in 'NHS' to rhyme with 'under too much stress'

Grace: And it's kind of annoying you how the whole crowd is cheering

Tom: Actually howling at certain points to be like *yes*, I *share* those political views. But you're like come on, this is not that astute

Anna: You pull out your picnic bag, open the hummus pot, and transfer the baggy into your bumbag

Max: Give it a lick first

Anna: What?

Max: Lick the humous off the baggy and put it into your bumbag

Anna: OK. And your picnic stuff looks really unappealing now because it's been in the hot van, so you're thinking you're going to chuck it away and buy something else. There's a smell of meat floating through the air up to your nostrils from the nearby burger stand. You inhale deeply

Grace: And yeah, you think. You could be into that

Max: You picture onions frying and your stomach grumbles in response. You think about going over to get one. But you realise that it really depends how much beef there is in the burgers, and there isn't a way to ask that question that wouldn't be awkwardly rude, so

Grace: You decide against it, setting your mind on the pizza stand next to it

**Anna/
Tom:** Or the vegan stand

Max: Burger

Grace: No, you choose the pizza stand, and you get up to buy a slice, when this guy, part of your group of friends / though

Max: Though you probably wouldn't call him a friend on individual terms

Anna: But he's friends with someone you know who invited him to the Facebook event

Tom: Says he's hungry too. Which is kind of annoying, but you reason that you might as well get past that awkward stage with him now since later you'll probably be rubbing his hands going, 'yes, yes, yes, oh my god, these feel so gorgeous'

Anna: 'I have so much respect for like, everything you do, and I wish we'd got to know each other earlier'

BREACH

Grace: You make your way over to the pizza stand with him, and make a sort of token gesture towards conversation – which makes him feel like he can get uncomfortably close and start talking to you

Tom: At you

Max: Spitting at you, about his new job, and as far as you can make out / it's basically

Grace: It's basically copywriting for some sort of agency, but he's weirdly really into it because the company he works for go on like, weekend bonding trips to Center Parcs

Tom: You wait for the pizza man to make his overpriced margherita, which essentially looks like a glorified cheese on toast

Grace: And the guy's telling you about this thing the company do every Thursday before work, where they have a *rave*

Tom: The pizza man hands you a sad looking slice

Anna: A breakfast rave, in a converted warehouse down the street from the office

Tom: You take a bite

Anna: Except instead of drugs or alcohol, they drink raw green vegetable smoothies and give each other massages

Tom: It's synthetic cheese balancing on a thin layer of sauce and thick white bread. It's surprisingly good

Grace: 'Because dancing sets you up for the day and makes you just that bit more focused, you know?'

Anna: And he's like, 'I guess that's like this, isn't it?'

Grace: And you look at his irritating, earnest face with his media moustache, and you're thinking / Oh my god

Anna: Oh my god no, it really isn't

Grace: But you can't twist your tongue into the words that explain why.

Carol Damaged (Ex-Traveller)
Carol's home, Daventry

Grace: How do you feel about the term the 'Battle of the Beanfield'?

Carol: I hate it! I don't like the Battle of the Beanfield being called the Battle of the Beanfield. I think a battle is between two groups of people equally armed, with equal intentions to hurt the other – and that's not what that day was at all. We were going to start the 1985 Stonehenge Free Festival with the intention of, yeah, putting on a festival for the working class people of Britain – and we were stopped violently by the police, by the army and by the state.

Grace: And if you were going to try and, say, re-enact the events of that day, what would you choose to act out?

Carol: OK, yeah, if I were to re-enact it, I suppose one of the major things is that police helicopter. Just the way that they hovered above us, the noise of it, the alien voice saying 'come out of your vehicles and be processed, no one will get hurt' – while you're surrounded by your friends bleeding, screaming, traumatised, trying to find their children, trying to save their dogs, trying to look after each other.

The picture of sort of, strong capable men being battered to the ground, especially hard because they were strong and capable, you know – the way that they attacked the people that they perceived to be the leaders amongst us. Um, my memories of the day are in cartoon form really.

Grace: And what were the police like to deal with at the Beanfield?

Carol: They used batons, and they used rocks, and they used bits of wood that they'd picked up. And I did see armed police that day – and I have been on record to say I'd seen armed police that day.

And they were also waiting for re-enforcements from Wiltshire, and the re-enforcements that turned up were soldiers – they were young soldiers. Because the police that we were dealing with were the same police that had been used in the miners' strikes, so they were in their thirties, they all had dodgy porntaches, they wore their uniform in a certain way – and the re-enforcements turned up and they were all seventeen, eighteen-year-old boys with soldier's haircuts. And they all wore their uniform in a very different way. Half of them had no numbers, most of them had no numbers, the boiler suits that they were wearing didn't have... it covered their lapels if they did have numbers. So they were, yeah, you couldn't, you couldn't go, 'PC 371 assaulted me'. The chap that, sort of, really assaulted me, I, you know, I don't know who he was.

Grace: And do you think any of the police officers who were there that day still think about it?

Carol: I actually met a police officer that was at the Beanfield, while I was sitting in a lay-by for a convoy of our vehicles to turn up, and he was sat on a police motorbike. And the thing with police cyclists is they really like their bikes, they're sort of 'cyclist first, policeman second'.

So we started talking about the bike, then we started talking about things in common, and then he sort of said, 'Well actually, I was at the Beanfield' – and I said, well, 'So was I'. And he got really upset. And, er, his story – he told me his story. So his story was that a few years earlier he'd been in the armed forces, and um, in some conflict somewhere he'd lost his friend at sort of – as far as I could work out – seventeen, eighteen. And when he'd got to the Beanfield, because of the violence, and because of the smells and the noise of the breaking glass and the screams, he'd flash-backed.

And when he came too, he was stood on the back of somebody's bus, with a big piece of two-by-four, and he was swinging it around and hitting police officers as well as travellers. And he said, literally, that's the moment he came too. He didn't realise that he'd flash-backed until he was aware of where he was, and what was happening. And, you know, there's palls of smoke going up and like I say, glass smashing, and people screaming and running round, and dogs barking, and shouting, and the police shouting from the police helicopter.

It was just one of those moment in time really. We both – it was just – yeah we just, we met

75

without, you know, he lost his uniform whilst speaking to me, you know, not physically, but he lost that. I lost my hippy uniform, and we were just two humans meeting on a, you know, on a level. And um, well we hugged each other actually. 'Cause he was crying, and obviously it was, it was only a couple of years after the Beanfield. And it took me quite a few years to be able to hear a police helicopter without having the same thing – without having my heart rate go, and without, you know, basically having flashbacks of *that*. So I understood – I understood that it wasn't something he necessarily had control over when he was being violent that day.

22:00

Tom: 10 pm. You're back with the group now

Grace: And it's a relief to no longer be one-on-one

Anna: Because there's only so much you can say about Center Parcs

Grace: And you're all walking around the stones. You've only ever seen them from far away, and now you're amongst them you see that they actually are / quite big

Tom: Really big, and sort of impressive. And one of them looks like it has a face carved into it

Grace: If you squint

Anna: A movement catches your eye and you look up, to see a man on top of one of the stones

Tom: He's running

Anna: Actually running, along the circle

Tom: A crowd forms underneath, cheering him on, and a second group, in hi-vis jackets, is running towards him. He's stark naked, standing on the / edge

Anna: Teetering on the edge, and then he launches himself to the next one and sits down. His legs dangle off the side and you're transfixed. But then you picture him falling – imagine his body crashing against the rock as he falls, and you think – if he dies, you'll have had to watch someone die

Tom: You turn away and walk up to another stone.
Look at its surface. It's weathered

Anna: Mossy, smoothed

Grace: Smoothed, yeah, by all the hands that have
touched it

Anna: You reach out. Cold to your fingertips

Tom: Security are trying to talk the man down from
the precipice

Anna: You spread your hand and press your palm
against the surface, trying to get / inside the
moment

Grace: Trying to think about the ways in which this is
/ significant

Anna: Meaningful. Picturing all the other people
from the past who've touched it. Like, er, Celts
painted in blue

Grace: Roman soldiers in silver and red. Rotten-
toothed peasants

Anna: A Victorian woman, who you realise is
actually Gemma Arterton out of the BBC *Tess
of the d'Urbervilles*

Tom: The man's scaling down the rock face now,
and the crowd scatters

Anna: 'Can you feel it?' Djembe-friend is asking

Tom: The one with the harem trousers

Anna: She's jamming her forehead against a rock like she's trying to force her way inside, like some sort of reverse birth. 'Can you?'

Grace: She means ... the *energy*

Anna: Anything about energy is instantly annoying, but you tentatively press your hand to the stone. Nothing. You feel ridiculous, but try to humour her by saying / 'yeah'

Tom: 'Yeah, yeah man – there's so much history here.' Even though your only sense of that history is something vaguely medieval

Grace: 'You do know how the stones got here, don't you?' she says, wide-eyed

Tom: She starts talking about a war. There's always a war. Something about a battle between the Angles and Saxons, right here on Salisbury Plain

Anna: And King Aurelius, that's King Arthur's father, she's explaining

Grace: King Aurelius led the Angles into battle and won, but the Saxons had killed a lot of his soldiers

Tom: So Aurelius decided to build a monument to mark the battle

Anna: Like a war memorial

Tom: 'But a / henge'

Grace: 'A henge,' she says. Whatever that is. So he summoned Merlin, who conjured a henge from a Giant's fortress, at the top of Mount Kilamajanjo

Anna: Kilima … Calamari?

Tom: Er, a mountain, she can't remember what it's called. 'Wait'

Grace: 'No wait'

Tom: She stops, confused

Anna: 'Actually I don't think it was that, sorry. I feel like the story involves an old lady's garden in Ireland'

Tom: She gets back into the flow

Anna: 'Yeah, so Merlin summoned the devil to get the stones for him, and the devil tricked this Irish woman to steal the stones off her. For the king, King Aurelius, Arthur's father'

Tom: Your mind is spinning with images again

Grace: Digital images

Anna: Sunlight on metal

Grace: Images of images

Anna: Blood on grass

Tom: Her story's jumping from one Wikipedia page to the next. You can't quite piece it together

Anna: She's starting to grate on you now and you're wondering like, how you're even friends with this person

Grace: And you're suddenly very conscious of your outstretched hand, which is still awkwardly stroking the stone

Tom touches the air.

Tom: You're like, 'right yeah, those / vibrations. I can feel it right ... *here*'

Anna: 'Vibrations, right'

Grace: You pull back your hand and decide to stop pretending

Tom: You were more into the pizza you ate earlier, and you're starting to feel like a bit of a fake.

Nottingham Medieval Re-enactment Society
Dorothy's bedroom, Leamington Spa

The sound of Skype connecting.

Billy: How much research do you do before a battle re-enactment, and how important is it to be historically accurate?

Kate: If you're re-enacting with an organisation, which most people do because it gives you insurance and it means that someone else sets the shows up for you, then there'll be a guidebook basically – that says 'you can wear this, but you can't wear this, because this is the evidence.' And obviously sometimes the evidence isn't clear, so you have different interpretations. It usually depends between the groups that you re-enact with what the accepted level of authenticity is – and to be honest a lot of it's best guess anyway, so you walk a line, I think.

Tom: And how might it be different if you were
staging a re-enactment of a battle that
happened only thirty years ago, like the Battle
of the Beanfield?

[*Concrete Walls* – **Fever Ray**]

Kate: Like medieval history, there's probably not
one truth about what happened that day –
there's lots of people's different accounts. So
you're probably going to have to take a side.
But when there's living humans involved, then
that's going to be so much more fraught with
issues than it is with medieval life, where no
one's around to care.

Max: How important is it that you re-enact a battle
on the exact site where it took place?

Peter: From an emotional perspective, it seems
incredibly important. I don't know about
everyone else, but there is a weirdly strong
feeling when you stand on a field, on the actual
battlefield. It's a very – it goes beyond a sort
of intellectual level, where you're interested
in educating or giving an experience to the
public, and it turns it into a kind of experience
for you … which is probably completely false.

Anna: And how does it feel if you're re-enacting an imbalanced battle – like if one side has weapons, and the other is unarmed?

Peter: The difficulty with portraying things like that is it makes you feel completely awful, if you do it with a very high degree of seriousness. And if you don't do it with a very high degree of seriousness, you don't feel awful – but it all seems farcical.

Kate: Yeah, it gets a bit pantomime, and you don't really convey any message. Except 'this is a silly show!' – which isn't what we're really out to do.

Ellice: Do you feel like you're playing a character during a re-enactment – and if so, how do you get into that character?

Peter: When you're actually fighting, you have to in some ways become a character, because you have to be able to put forward the kind of aggression and level of violence that these events involved. So unless you're, at least to a certain extent, imagining yourself into a character in the past, you can't really put forward that level of viciousness, and anger, and fear.

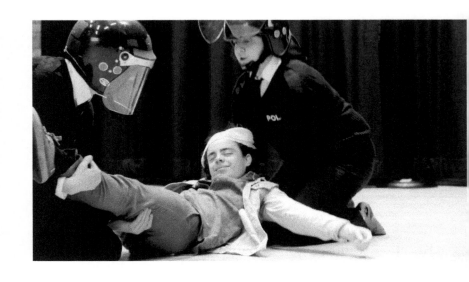

Grace: So do you ever find yourself getting emotional on the battlefield, like having a sort of emotional outburst?

Peter: Well, people end up in fights reasonably... not often, but they do. People do end up thumping the shit out of each other. It's often over silly things. People get very, very hyped up.

Max: Do you have any final words of advice for us before we do our re-enactment?

Peter: Be careful.

All laugh.

01:00

Max: It's around 1 am. You've got that tingly feeling in your stomach after dropping a bomb that makes you feel like you might need to do a massive shit

Ellice: Yeah, so you turn to the group to make your excuses. They don't notice. You pick up your bumbag and clip it round your waist

Max: You walk through the floodlit dark towards the line of portaloos, with that Glastonbury stench that you secretly think is a bit nice

Ellice: You get in line behind a Hare Krishna and you both shuffle slowly towards the blue-tinged smell

–

Max: The Hare Krishna opens the door and nods at you, rubbing sanitiser in his hands

Ellice: You close the door behind you and turn the lock

Max: You sit down and put your chin in your hands, tapping your toes. The tingling intensifies

Ellice: You focus on the red and green of the lock as you inhale. Tense

Max: Eyes straining, body clenching

Ellice: And wait for the release. It comes

Max: It's shit

Ellice: Literally. But not much, just three rabbit droppings which don't justify the cramps and that disappoints you

Max: Maximum effort to minimum volume

Ellice: Awful ratio. You think you might have more in you but it doesn't look like it's coming out. It's just an incomplete poo

Max: You're not even sure if you're coming up – you just feel a bit / anxious

Ellice: Anxious and a bit sick

Max: You're done here

Ellice: And as you button up, your mouth dries, and the dark blue light intensifies

[*Now's the Only Time I Know* – Fever Ray]

Max: Is it coming?

Ellice: You think so. You swallow hard and brace for the rush. But then you spot your face in the tiny scratchy mirror on the door. Your jaw is sliding out, pupils like black plates and glitter sweating off and you look ... well, you look stunning

Max: But it doesn't feel like it's hitting you

Ellice   Right, it's frustrating. There's a / weird frustration about that

Max: Weird frustration. So you open your bumbag, fish out the baggy and have another dab

Ellice: Chemical, metallic, like the liquid in a thermometer, / thermometer juice

Max: Thermometer juice. There's a knock at the door and an alien voice says / 'excuse me'

Ellice: 'Excuse me, there are actually other people waiting to get in there, please'

Max: You might have been in here longer than you thought. You step outside and walk past a middle-aged woman with a child, about seven or eight, whose eyes bore into your soul

Ellice: OK, they don't bore into your soul, but you do think it's a bit weird that there's a kid here

–

Max: 2 am

Ellice: You bump straight into Center Parcs guy from before, who grabs you by the shoulders in a sweaty hug. He keeps asking if you're having a good night, without waiting for a reply. His eyes are wide like, like craters

Max: The impact sites of a serotonin meteor

Ellice: But less poetic

Max: He's / 'so happy he found you', but he's looking around and through you

BREACH

Ellice: 'Happy he found you'

Max: He drags you into the centre of the throng of sweaty bodies. You hear different drums beating an irregular rhythm and find your steps are always out of sync

Ellice: But mentally you're above again, watching. You close your eyes and move with him

Max: You feel his cold skin against you as your sweat mingles. You know it's gross, because you know / it's sweat

Ellice: It's sweat, but it feels quite nice – like a waterfall in a shampoo advert. So you fight the urge to pull away

Max: You mimic his dancing and he presses his forehead against yours. He shouts so loudly that you can't hear what he's trying to say. He's rambling. Maybe praying. You strain to listen

Ellice: 'I can still see your face when I close my eyes'

Max: 'Sorry, what?'

Ellice: 'I said, do you know how it is that Stevie Wonder went blind?'

Max: 'No, I don't'

Ellice: 'Not enough oxygen – we've got to breathe'

Max: 'Cool, well I am breathing', you say, and

Ellice rubs her fingers together.

Ellice: 'It's like my fingers are clitorises'

Max: 'OK, well'

Ellice: 'No seriously, clitorises – CLITORI'

Landowner
Rehearsal Room, Milburn House, Warwick University

The sound of a phone ringing.

Ellice *(as
Landowner)*: Hello?

Dorothy: Hi, I'm just calling because – I'm a student
from Warwick University, and … I think I
just spoke to your son, ██████ –

Ellice *(as
Landowner)*: Right.

Dorothy: And basically, I'm calling because I'm
currently doing a theatre and film project
which is to do with the Battle of the
Beanfield…

Ellice *(as
Landowner)*: Oh right, yeah. That was before we moved
here.

Dorothy: Ah, well it's um – I'm sure you know, it
took place in the field just below or just
above yours –

Ellice *(as
Landowner)*: Yeah.

Dorothy: And so basically we're going to try and
stage a very small-scale re-enactment
in this field, in the Beanfield, although
I haven't managed to get through to Mr
████████████████, who's the owner of
that land.

Ellice *(as*
Landowner):   I can't say I'm terribly keen on that –
because although your part might be well
organised, I don't know who else it would
attract to the area. It's been very peaceful
since we've been here, but apparently it
wasn't before, so I would be reluctant to
sort of stir that up again.

Dorothy: Just to reinforce, we're not looking to stir
up any trouble –

Ellice *(as*
Landowner):   Yes, but there used to be a lot of trouble
here apparently, so I would be perfectly
happy for all that to just stay that in the
past, I'm afraid, now. I can just imagine,
whoever it was, the trouble beforehand,
I can imagine this attracting unsavoury
elements ... But I don't know.

Dorothy: It'll be a very small-scale re-enactment,
which will literally just be using the land
so that it's, kind of, revisiting a historical
site –

Ellice *(as*
Landowner):   And I think I'm going to have to say no.
As I say, I'm not that keen on it.

Dorothy: OK, thank you very much for speaking to
me, thanks for your help.

Ellice *(as*
Landowner):   OK, bye.

Dorothy: Have a nice weekend, bye.

–

Grace: I've got a suggestion.

Dorothy: That we go there anyway, and we tell
               them to – ?

Grace: That we call the hotel. So maybe if we ask
               the hotel in the field next to them –

Dorothy: I don't think we should even be asking
               anyone, I think we should just go. I think
               they'll say no, and then I think they'll turf
               us off, *and* it will be potential warrant for
               arrest, for trespassing.

Re-enactment
Wiltshire

[*Mirie It Is* – **Bishi**]

Mirie it is while sumer y-last / With
What this nicht is long / And ich with

gheles son / Oc nu neheth windes blast / And weder strong / Ei, ei!
el michel wrong / Soregh and murne and fast

Ellice: Hi

Andy: That [costume] is really worrying – I've just been looking over the photos

Tom: Hello

Dorothy: It's alright, they're not real police, they're all students. Shall we go? OK, do you want to jump in there?

Andy: Is that the Beanfield?

Dorothy: We guess. Because this field must be – I
think the one the other side of it is the
Beanfield …

Andy: What's this road we're on then?

Dorothy: We're on the B343 I think … and then in
parallel is the A303

Andy: I'm starting to wonder about the accuracy
of this map

The van pulls into the car park of the ▮▮▮▮▮ *Hotel.*
Dorothy *gets out and walks across to try and jump the fence
into an adjacent field. A man runs out of the building and
chases her.*

Ellice: Oh fuck

Grace: Does someone want to go and give her a
little bit of backup?

Billy: Yeah, but don't go in the police wear

Grace: He's running!

Tom: Yeah right, Andy and someone who's not
dressed as a policeman?

Billy: Yeah

Andy: He's saying it's not here

Grace: It is here. He's lying

Dorothy *gets back into the van.*

Dorothy: So he came over to me, and he said, 'what are you doing? You're on private property, get off' – tried to just kick me off. And I said, 'I'm just trying to work out where certain fields are.' And he went, 'that's not the Beanfield.' And then we started talking about it and he was like, 'you're trespassing, this is private property, off you go.' And I said, 'is there any way you could help me to find the Beanfield?'And he said, 'it's a very sore subject for everyone who lives around here'

Anna: He said 'there are raw rounds'

Dorothy: 'There are raw wounds, get off.' He said, 'I'm pretty sure you can ask any local around here and no one will know where it is, and no one will want to talk about it.' Ie. they don't want to talk about it, so

Billy: So leave?

Dorothy: So blissful ignorance. And so they're not going to tell us where it is. But I think that is it. He kept saying 'that's not the Beanfield', because obviously it is, and he said 'you can go and try a pub down there in the next village and they might know'. And I said, 'do you have any idea?' And he said 'no, no one knows.'

He said no one knows where it is

After driving around and finding another way into the field,

the cast get out of the van and warm up.

Dorothy: Alright, go! 3, 2, 1… Action. Action!

[*Seventeen Come Sunday (English Folk Song Suite)* – **Ralph Vaughan Williams**]

Carol
(voiceover): My memories of the day are in cartoon form really … [the police were] moving up the convoy and just smashing windows, getting hold of people by the hair, dragging them out through the broken glass

Carol
(voiceover): I was completely covered in glass from the window screen, because when it had gone through it had sat on the top of my jeans and things like that, so Jeanie and I sort of took our trousers off but all our stuff was in the back of the van

We couldn't find our clothes, so we just
literally just got a couple of sort of hippy
scarves and wrapped them around our waists
because it was so hot

Nick
(voiceover): It was extremely upsetting to see essentially
vulnerable people – men, women, children –
being attacked by grown men with big sticks,
and riot shields and helmets. It was an utterly
uneven battle

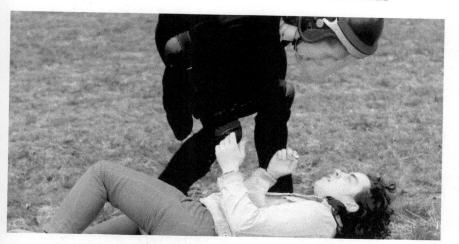

Carol
(voiceover): They battered my friend Mick to the floor. And they
screamed 'he's got something in his hand, he's got
something in his hand', and threw him to the floor,
turned his arm round, battered him until he let go of
it, it was a lighter. Then they picked Phil up off the
floor, walked him to the back of his home, opened the
door, lit it with his best friend's lighter, and made him
stand there and watch his home burn

Ruwan
(voiceover): Mothers of children distraught, trying to find out where their children were … because we'd taken them away

Carol
(voiceover):   [We were] dragged off to the bottom of the field, put into a riot wagon with a sergeant, or something like that. He sat us in the back of the van and pushed his legs ... leant in with his knee inside our crotches, leant forward and said 'You're not on a fucking picnic'

Ruwan
(voiceover):   When the vehicles were taken away – when
their homes were taken away – if they hadn't
been destroyed, they then were. And that was
done in the total cold light of day

Carol
(voiceover):   I got away from the police that had arrested me
and ran back up to where Jeanie was and I was just
like 'leave the dog, leave the dog', and I sort of put
myself over her and so we both got hit, and then
we managed to unlock the dog and the dog ran.
I walked over to the fence and I thought the police
were playing football. But they were … there was
a gang of about ten of them, and they were using a
dog as a football

Billy: Are you alright?

Grace: This is really fucking painful

Grace: Yeah, yeah, no, it's just the smack really hurt. And then the second smack really hurt, and like, it's really fucking brutal

Anna: Just with the, with the batons

Grace: Look it's fine, it's fine, but it's really fucking horrible

Anna: Just do it lightly

Ellice: We need to like, talk about it though

Dorothy: Is this the last scene?

Ellice: I don't know

Grace: No, because we've got to shoot it, haven't we?

Max: Are you OK?

Anna: Just do it like – when you're – with the batons – because it's stinging a bit

Billy: OK. OK

Grace: I didn't think I'd actually react this emotionally to it

Anna: Yeah

Grace: It's really fucking horrible

Grace *starts to cry.*

Ellice: Ok well look, let's stop then

Grace: No, you don't have to stop

Ellice: No, it doesn't matter – it's better to stop. Because otherwise it's going to come out in like a way that's dangerous

Grace: Ok, let's just do it again

Ellice: No, I think, honestly, it's better to take a minute

Max: Let's take five, like honestly, just take five

Dorothy: This is probably what they looked like. This is probably more accurate and more authentic

Grace: Yeah, I know

Dorothy: And it's horrible, but ... channel it, you know

Grace: Yeah

Billy: Use it

Dorothy: Yeah

Grace: It just like – actually brings out a lot of like, horror

Ellice: Yeah

Grace: It's like, very like, horrific

Max: It's because it's

Dorothy: Because we know that this is

Billy: Real

Dorothy: A real event.

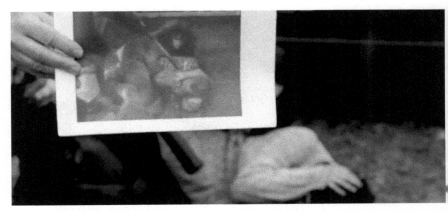

02:45

Dark stage, green screen.

__Anna__ enters and stands in its glow, holding a microphone which she speaks into.

Anna: 2:45 am.

You pull your face away from his sweaty palms, and your head flicks backwards. Regain balance as Stevie-Wonder-Center-Parcs-friend turns and disappears into the crowd. You're alone now, between different circles of dancers, and you strain to see what they're gathered around. It's a group of intensely absorbed drummers.

You step into the stones.

Haze. ***Tom*** *enters in police costume, holding a plank of two-by-four wood. He paces.*

[Let Me Down Gently – La Roux]

The dancers are wild-eyed, with round black pupils, and their skin is glowing and you're just watching them over a sea of pulsing bodies and moving heads. You feel a pang to be one of these wild-eyed pixies, to dance and glow with them. You want to get swept up in it, you want feet-pounding, sweat-dripping, all-encompassing joy.

You make a path through people, squeezing through sweaty bodies until you're with your new friends. You start clapping in time with

BREACH

them, moving your hips and stamping hard.
They all have face paint and glitter on their
cheeks, and they just look fucking glorious,
and their smiles burn and their eyes are
closed, like they're feeling without seeing.

You raise your hands and turn your face
up to the sky, picturing how the sun
will split it open in a few hours – willing
yourself to join them in that dancing
frenzy. Their bodies are pushing you from
side to side as they dance, but you just
close your eyes and smile.

Blackout. Strobe. **Tom** *begins swinging the plank around as if
hitting invisible people. This movement begins slowly and becomes
increasingly violent, building to a frenzy as* **Anna** *speaks.*

A surge of euphoria hits, moving through
your body fast and strong, and now you
just want to dance – no, you must dance.
You mindlessly follow the impulse, put
your head down as a smile stretches across
your face. You run your tongue down the
ridges that have formed down the sides of
your mouth – two roads that meet at the
grinding of teeth – and the drumming
seems to be getting faster and faster until
you're dancing like a fury, like a whirling
dervish, so hard and so fast that you can't
believe that these are actually your feet.

*Strobe stops. Lights very slowly – almost imperceptibly – begin
to come up, so that the very final moments are brightly lit.*

You have no idea how long you've been
dancing – time has become meaningless –

and the drums keep thumping around you
and through you, and you keep spinning.
You're spinning, and stamping, and
reaching for that release into the summer,
a new beginning where you'll actually
become yourself and live in the world and
not just pretend, and you think you might
be there.

Grace enters in bloodied traveller costume. She approaches
Tom and lifts his helmet visor, forcing him to look at her.

You're just short of an epiphany, when you
come to and realise how cold you now are.
You feel your arms drop lower, your feet
hit the ground gentler and you try to push
all thoughts away and get back that frenzy,
but you can't.

As *Anna* battles to be heard over the music, *Grace* wrestles
Tom's helmet off and he rips away her jacket. Exhausted
and out of breath, the two circle one another, never breaking
eye-contact. They gradually remove each layer of costume –
their own and one another's. When they are down to their
underwear, they stand facing each other among the discarded
clothes.

You're too aware of the goose pimples
covering your skin, the cold sweat running
down your back, and the blisters forming
on the soles of your feet.

You look at the faces around you, and
they're distant and glazed. You stop,
watching them all dance as their glitter
melts into sweat. Their glow cuts out, and

the drumming becomes white noise. You
step back and inhale deeply. Turn your
face up towards the clouds and in your
peripheral vision you can see the tops of
the rocks closing in on you. You're aware
of your heart thumping. You turn your
head, disoriented and bleary, and look for
a way out – pushing through the crowd
again, moving as spaces appear, and you
stagger out of the stones.

Weaving through people in yoga poses,
people chanting and singing, holding up
their phones, trying to break open the
moment and climb inside it, you find your
way to an empty patch of grass and collapse.

You feel the coolness of the dew on your
arms as you lie back, and rip out the grass
by the fistfull. The sweat that was pouring
off you before like a beautiful waterfall is
now freezing, clammy on your skin.

Your muscles are tingling. Looking up
at the sky, you realise that after all that
time waiting for the sun to come up, it's
now just suddenly bright. You don't know
where exactly the sun is, but the sky is
blue-grey and looks flat, and the grass
a violent synthetic green. You rub your
eyes, digging the heels of your hands into
them hard to adjust to the daylight. Birds
screech, and a news helicopter whirs
overhead, and you're thinking like

is this it?

WWW.OBERONBOOKS.COM

Follow us on www.twitter.com/@oberonbooks
& www.facebook.com/OberonBooksLondon